THE ARENA DISTRICT

A Neighborhood 170 Years in the Making

This volume is published by Nationwide Realty Investors, Ltd.,
a subsidiary of Nationwide Mutual Insurance Company.

© 2006, Nationwide Realty Investors
ISBN 0-977-6350-0-7

MANAGING EDITOR: Michelle Chippas, Nationwide Realty Investors

PROJECT MANAGER AND EDITOR: Nathan G. Kraft, Nationwide Realty Investors

RESEARCH: Ed Lentz, Pastfinders

COPYWRITING: Jaron Terry, APR, Jaron Terry Communications

DESIGN: Scott Adams Design Associates

PRINTED BY: West-Camp Press, Inc.

THE ARENA DISTRICT

A Neighborhood 170 Years in the Making

A DEVELOPMENT OF NATIONWIDE REALTY INVESTORS

This book is dedicated to those
who have made this neighborhood their own
in the past, present and future.

ALL GREAT NEIGHBORHOODS HAVE RICH HISTORIES, and the Arena District is no exception.

Since Columbus' earliest days, the area in and around what is now known as the Arena District has been a center of activity. These city blocks have witnessed waves of energy, from railroad workers and prisoners to farmers and early Irish settlers.

And after recent decades of sitting dormant, the area has again experienced a rebirth and a new wave of energy. The Arena District features the region's most popular sports, dining and entertainment venues, premier office space and is now home to hundreds of residents.

By painting a story through photos, this book provides a glimpse into the area's past and a look at its present. It is not intended to be a historic chronicle of everything that has happened here, nor is it a 'how-to' book outlining the perfect urban renaissance. Each page tells but one story of the many people and institutions who have contributed to the area's illustrious history.

Welcome to the Arena District.

BRIAN J. ELLIS
President and COO
Nationwide Realty Investors

1834 - 1997

EARLY COLUMBUS

HALFWAY THROUGH THE 19TH CENTURY, Columbus had grown far

beyond the frontier town that had been incorporated in 1816. With

a population of nearly 18,000, the capital city depicted in this 1854

lithograph is a faint echo of the humming, major metropolitan area

Columbus is today. Then known as North Public Lane, Nationwide

Boulevard marked the northern most boundary of the fledgling city.

This area, once a hub of manufacturing and transportation—and home

to the Ohio Penitentiary—is known today as the Arena District.

OHIO PENITENTIARY

For 150 years until its closing in 1984, the Ohio Penitentiary was home to hundreds of thousands of prisoners. For some the stay was short; for many it was a lifetime; and still others never left.

The "Pen" opened as a source of civic pride with 189 prisoners in 1834. It was located on a 22-acre plot of what was then considered the city's fringe on West Spring Street between West Street and Dennison Avenue (now known as Neil Avenue).

The ornate, fortress-like limestone Administration Building ran nearly the length of Spring Street and a distinctive 24-foot wall surrounded the site, which was built at a cost of more than $93,000, including an estimated $78,000 of inmate labor.

In 1877, an additional floor and new façade featuring a heavy masonry cornice were added. Punctuated at regular intervals by glyphs, or moldings, the front view is also interrupted by twin towers, as well as the jutting portico of the administration building.

Historian Martin Fornshell described the Pen as standing alone "in the imposing and massive grandeur of its severe and stately front—a silent and frowning warning to the observer of the majesty of the law and the consequences which are sure to follow and overtake those who insult or violate its imperial dignity and sovereign mandates."

A 1908 account of the Ohio Pen that refers to the stone and steel structure as an "acre of sorrow" details many sad incidences, such as the 1849 cholera epidemic that claimed one quarter of the prison's 423 inmates. Although the practice of whipping was abolished in 1844, punishment by dunking, time in the "sweatbox" and electrical shock were still employed. By the late 1880s however, the Ohio Pen gained a national reputation as a model prison, thanks to reforms instituted by Warden E.G. Coffin, who served until 1900. He not only did away with inhumane punishments, but was lauded in Columbus newspapers for his view that, "A hard box to sleep on and bread and water to eat will cause them to behave themselves." Despite having responded to national prison reform efforts, discontent and disaster continued to haunt the Pen.

1968 Riots

In August of 1968, Ohio Highway Patrolmen enter the Ohio Pen to quell rioting. Nine guards had been taken hostage by prisoners demanding reform. Five inmates were killed in the 28-hour stand-off that ended as law enforcement officers used explosives to blow holes in the south wall and the roof. This incident, a follow-up to riots in June of that same year, would convince officials that the prison could no longer be part of Columbus' skyline.

1930 Easter Monday Fire

The worst prison fire in U.S. history, which claimed the lives of 322 inmates, took place at the Ohio Penitentiary. The bodies of the inmates who died in the 1930 Easter Monday Fire were taken to a temporary morgue in the horticulture building at the Ohio State Fairgrounds.

The fire started in New Hall, which had been constructed atop a former prison cemetery along the west flank of the prison. This is the present site of the Neil Avenue parking garage. Unlike other buildings, New Hall was somewhat like a large barn with walls of stone and a wooden roof covered with slate. All prisoners had been locked in for the night when the fire – set earlier in the day by inmates who touched a candle flame to oily rags – burst forth. An investigation revealed that guards had not been trained to deal with fire, leading to the fatal delay in freeing the prisoners. Of the three inmates accused of starting the fire, two later committed suicide.

Old Sparky

Capital punishment has been a part of Ohio's justice system since the state's birth in 1803. Starting in 1885, all Ohio executions were required to take place – by hanging – at the Ohio Penitentiary. In 1897, the electric chair, nicknamed "Old Sparky" and said to be a more humane form of execution, was erected directly under the trap of the old gallows, so that the condemned would die in exactly the same spot as those who went before. A total of 315 persons – including three women – were executed at the Pen.

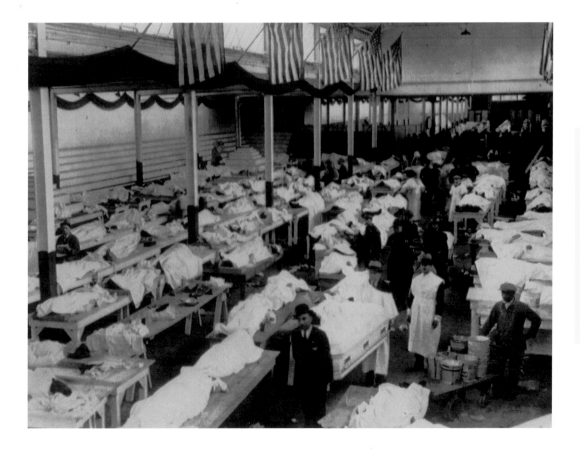

Bankers' Row

In 1894, a local newspaper reporter discovered that Ohio Penitentiary prisoners were still being locked in sweat boxes for punishment. However, well-connected white-collar prisoners were housed in larger, airy cells in an area informally dubbed "Banker's Row." Cells on the ground floor were highly coveted because climbing stairs was inconvenient and, in the days before air conditioning, were considerably cooler than higher cells.

Sam Sheppard

One of the most famous prisoners was Dr. Sam Sheppard, who served ten years for the 1954 murder of his wife. Sentenced to life in prison, he was released after his attorney, F. Lee Bailey, convinced a federal district court that he had not received a fair trial. A subsequent trial found him not guilty. In 1997, DNA evidence strongly suggested that Mrs. Sheppard had been killed by Richard Eberling, who died in prison while serving time for the murder of another woman.

John Hunt Morgan

Brigadier General John Hunt Morgan, known as "The Thunderbolt of the Confederacy," made a daring escape from the Ohio Pen on November 27, 1863. Thwarted and captured during a raid through Ohio, General Morgan and his men, known as "Morgan's Raiders," had been imprisoned in cells measuring only 3'x 6' and 7' high. Captain Thomas Henry Hines, mastermind of the escape, had discovered a ventilation passageway. After exploratory digging with dining hall knives, he discovered that the cell floor rested atop a brick arch covering an air chamber below.

Digging in shifts over a period of just a few weeks, Morgan's men made their way through 26 inches of material to enter the chamber, and spent another week chiseling through the Pen's granite foundation. Over the next two weeks, they tunneled under the jail yard to where they would later emerge just feet from the 20 foot outer wall. Gen. Morgan and his men made their bold escape by scaling the wall with a sturdy rope fashioned out of braided bedclothes.

On September 3, 1864, less than one year after his escape, Morgan was felled by a Union bullet, in Greeneville, Tennessee. The Morgan escape cell remained a popular stop on the Ohio Pen tour until the old East Cellblock was demolished. The lock is on display at the Corrections Training Academy in the Orient Correctional Complex.

O. Henry

Prolific American short story writer O. Henry, whose most famous works include "The Gift of the Magi," was incarcerated in the Ohio Penitentiary from 1898 to 1901. O. Henry was the pseudonym of William Sydney Porter, who was convicted of embezzlement. While serving three years of his five-year federal sentence, O. Henry began writing short stories. According to some sources, Porter took his pseudonym from a guard, Orrin Henry. According to others, he took it from the name of French pharmacist Etienne-Ossian Henry, which he found in the U.S. Dispensatory, a reference book he used while working in the prison pharmacy. He went on to author more than 600 short stories before alcoholism and ill health caught up with him. In 1910, O. Henry died of cirrhosis at age 48 in New York City. He had 23 cents to his name. After O. Henry left the Ohio Pen, the ball diamond in the prisoner recreation area was named for him. From the 1940s through mid-1960, softball teams came from all over to play the prison's AAA softball team, the "Hurricanes." His work, characterized by ironic twists and surprise endings, is published in several collections and numerous anthologies.

The Ohio Penitentiary, as it appeared in 1977, was in deep disrepair. Damage caused by fires and rioting prisoners, as well as neglect due to a lack of funding and interest, allowed the once stately structures to deteriorate beyond the point of salvage. At the same time, One Nationwide Plaza rises in the distance, marking the beginning of urban revitalization in the area, along with construction of the Ohio Center, hotels and – eventually – Nationwide Arena and the Arena District.

Having faced criticism from reformers since the early 1900s and having been the site of numerous tragic incidences, U.S. District Court Judge Robert Duncan ordered that the prison be closed by 1983. The men pictured above are being escorted out of the Pen on their way to the Southern Ohio Correctional Facility in Lucasville.

In its final years of operation the Pen served as a maximum security facility and medical reception point for prisoners deemed mentally ill, sick or unable to be rehabilitated. When the penitentiary finally closed in August, 1984, it was one of the oldest continuously operating inner-city maximum security facilities in the nation.

EARLY UNION DEPOTS

First Union Depot

The first railroad car entered Columbus' Union Depot in 1850. The Columbus and Xenia pulled into the city's first train station, constructed approximately where the Hyatt Regency is today. High Street is seen in the foreground. Naghten Street, which was then Columbus' north boundary and today is known as Nationwide Boulevard, runs adjacent to the building. The depot was in a rural, unpopulated area, a mere 50 feet from High and Naghten streets. This first station, which served just 25 years, featured two octagonal cupolas rising 10 feet above a central ridge pole that supported a wooden roof, which often was endangered by flying sparks from locomotives. Passengers crossed the muddy yard via wooden planks to access three tracks that ran through the center of the structure.

Second Union Depot

After the Civil War, Columbus citizens began complaining about conditions at the original depot. Passengers' clothing were often soiled when boarding trains as they had to walk across a muddy expanse. Further, the grade crossing on High Street was a nuisance, as trains frequently blocked traffic. A new and larger structure completed in February, 1875, boasted a 160 foot tunnel – centered under High Street – that allowed vehicular and pedestrian traffic to cross under the tracks. This three-story, red brick structure was thought to be quite grand. Italianate Revival Mansard roofs graced either end, while six round-arched openings on the west wall served as train portals. A cobblestone driveway bordered by a brick walkway led passengers from High Street to a canopied entrance.

UNION STATION

Columbus had become an important industrial and commercial center by the 1890s. Passenger and freight traffic through the Columbus Union Depot had become extremely heavy, as train travel was still the only means of traveling beyond horse-drawn range. Columbus' third Union Depot, opened in 1897, can be seen behind the beautiful beaux-arts arcade, housing shops and serving as a grand entryway to the actual train station. This depot, designed by famed architect Daniel Burnham, afforded greater access and was built in conjunction with a wide viaduct that carried High Street traffic over the tracks. The arcade, with its beautiful arches (one of which stands today at the apex of McFerson Commons), was built atop the viaduct.

LIFE AROUND UNION STATION

After construction, the new Union Station was a tremendous success. And the blocks immediately surrounding the station became the equivalent of a public square—a place that everyone knew. Hundreds of thousands passed through over the years, coming and going from wars, migrations, and the daily business of American life. Left, the beautiful Beaux-Arts Classicism-style arches of the Union Station Arcade are visible during the 1910 streetcar strike that halted public transportation in the city.

The Man Behind the Arcade

Daniel Burnham was an internationally-renowned American architect and urban planner who designed the Union Station Arcade. Responsible for the 1893 Columbian Exhibition in Chicago, he also designed Chicago's famous Montauk and LaSalle buildings. A member of the Chicago School of Architecture, Burnham also designed Columbus' Wyandotte Building, the first steel-framed skyscraper in Columbus. It is reported that Burnham, who died at age 66 in 1912, once said, "Make no little plans. They have no magic to stir men's blood and probably will themselves not be realized."

The Arch City

This photo, looking north on High Street near Union Station, illustrates why Columbus was once known as the Arch City. First constructed from wood in 1888, and later replaced by spans of steel, numerous arches marked the 100th anniversary of the first settlement of the Northwest Territory. Electric trolley cars and horse-drawn buggies shared the thoroughfare. Despite their drawing tourists and officials from numerous other cities, the arches were removed to make way for "modern" light poles in 1914. In 2002, Columbus could once again call itself the Arch City. New steel arches featuring lighted globes were constructed in the Short North, dotting the High Street landscape from Interstate 670 to just north of Fifth Street.

A Grade Above

Davidson Hotel

The Davidson Hotel once stood at the site of today's Sensenbrenner Park – at the corner of High and what is now East Nationwide Boulevard. One of the better small hotels in Columbus from 1878 to 1916, the Davidson was a favorite among more affluent travelers. It later operated as The Waldo.

Looking south on High Street, a man walks atop the viaduct, constructed in conjunction with the third rendition of Union Station. The viaduct, which spanned the width of High Street, allowed trains that once halted street and pedestrian traffic to proceed without inconvenience. The grade of High Street was raised by building massive brick vaults under the street and trucking in tons of fill dirt. Many businesses lining the thoroughfare found that their second floors became their new street level entrances. On the west side of High Street (left), the Davidson Hotel at the corner of High and Naghten streets rises above other businesses and hotels in the area.

A HUB OF ACTIVITY

In April 1898, the 3rd Ohio Volunteer Infantry was organized in Columbus to serve in the Spanish American War. Company B, from Springfield, Ohio, marches south on North High Street after debarking at Union Station (visible in background).

A Presidential Visit

President Woodrow Wilson was among many luminaries to visit Columbus' Union Station. He arrived in September of 1919 to rally support for the League of Nations. William Oxley Thompson (in profile), who was president of The Ohio State University from 1900 to 1925, accompanied Wilson in his touring car to Ohio's Statehouse. Wilson suffered his debilitating stroke just weeks after his visit to Columbus, where he made one of forty speeches on an 8,000-mile nationwide tour. The Union Station Arcade is visible in the rear of the shot.

Shriner's Parade

The "Sells Brothers Great European Circus and Menagerie" loaned elephants for the Shriner's parade along North High Street in this 1898 photograph. The Sells brothers left their home in what is today Dublin, Ohio, in the years following the Civil War. They operated the second-largest circus in the United States by the end of the 19th century. Their "7 Elephant Railroad" traveled by rail throughout the States from spring to fall, when it would return to its winter headquarters in the village of Sellsville, located across the river from The Ohio State University.

Lincoln's Funeral Train

After his assassination in April, 1865, President Abraham Lincoln made his final journey home to Springfield, Illinois, in a grand funeral procession that retraced the 1,654-mile route he traveled as President-elect in 1861. The train arrived at Columbus' Union Station in the morning of April 29. The coffin was then carried in a horse drawn hearse to the Statehouse. There, several thousands of Ohioans came to mourn the fallen president, viewed by many as the country's savior after the Civil War.

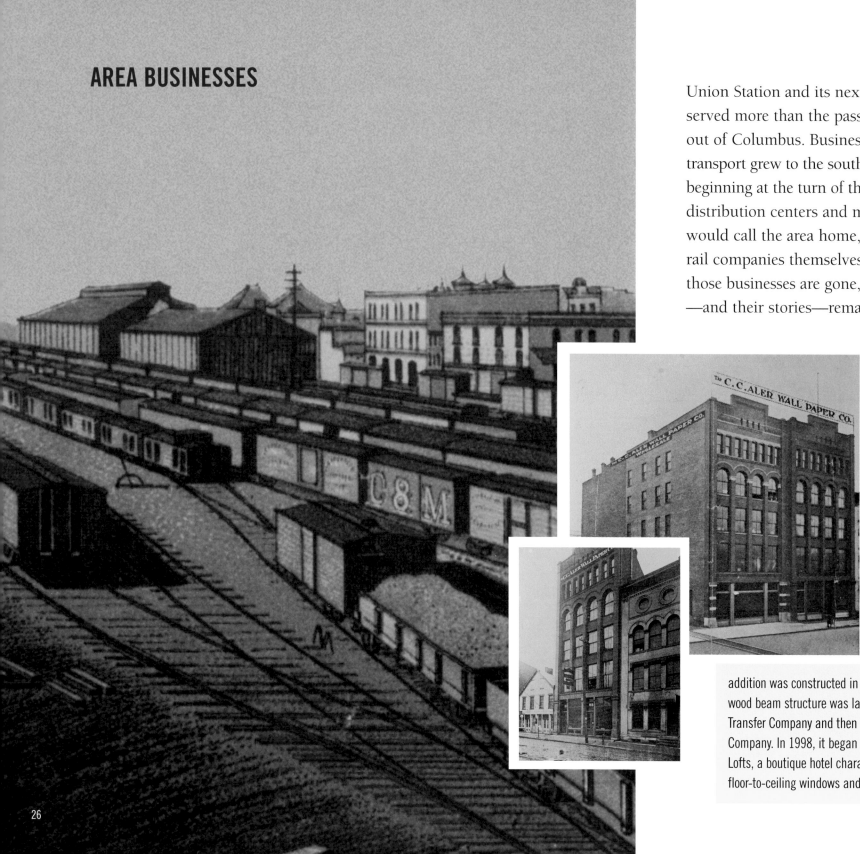

AREA BUSINESSES

Union Station and its nexus of railroad tracks served more than the passengers heading in and out of Columbus. Businesses reliant upon rail transport grew to the south and east of the station beginning at the turn of the century. Warehouses, distribution centers and manufacturing facilities would call the area home, some operated by the rail companies themselves. While nearly all of those businesses are gone, some of the buildings —and their stories—remain.

C.C. Aler Wallpaper Co.

Today, the Lofts Hotel occupies this 55 E. Nationwide Boulevard building that was built in 1882 in the midst of Columbus' bustling warehouse district by wall covering manufacturer Charles Aler. An addition was constructed in 1900. The sturdy brick and wood beam structure was later occupied by the Columbus Transfer Company and then the Carr Plumbing Supply Company. In 1998, it began its transformation into the Lofts, a boutique hotel characterized by exposed brick, floor-to-ceiling windows and tall, dramatic doorways.

Dean & Barry Paint Co.

In 1906, the Dean & Barry Paint Company moved offices and manufacturing facilities into this complex situated just east of the Ohio State Penitentiary. As the company grew, the complex expanded with new buildings in 1929, 1938 and 1969, all of which were designed to complement the original. After the paint company relocated in the early 1990s, each building was restored to its architectural roots. Known today as Marconi Square, the complex houses traditional offices and creative display space for design-related businesses.

A & P Building

The Great Atlantic & Pacific Tea Company was a formidable force in the local grocery business, competing with giants such as Kroger and Big Bear from the late 1800s through 1978. To service its growing store base, A & P opened this grocery warehouse at Neil Avenue and Spring Street in 1926 at a cost of $500,000. After A & P ceased its Ohio operations, the warehouse served as a general storage facility, most recently for commercial baking equipment.

BUGGY CAPITAL OF THE WORLD

With nearly two dozen buggy manufacturers operating in the city by the turn of the century, Columbus was known as the *Buggy Capital of the World.* By 1900, the Columbus Buggy Company (left) employed 800. Today this is the site of The Buggyworks, housing lofts, condominiums and offices, on what is now West Nationwide Boulevard. This building was also once the home of Union Fork & Hoe Company, predecessor to Union Tools.

Combination Phaeton

At the height of its business shortly after the turn of the century, the Columbus Buggy Company's best-selling vehicle was the Combination Phaeton. Within a few short years however, the company discovered it could not compete with Henry Ford's automobile and closed business in 1913.

Iron Buggy Company

This simple frame shop, located at the corner of Hickory Alley and High Street – where Nationwide's headquarters sit today – once housed the Iron Buggy Company, later known as the Columbus Buggy Company. By 1890, the Columbus Buggy Company was not only the largest manufacturer in Columbus, but also the largest buggy company in the world.

Eddie Rickenbacker

First as a mechanic and then as a test driver for the Columbus Buggy Company, war hero and Columbus native Eddie Rickenbacker developed a reputation as a fearless and fortunate driver of fast cars. The first automobile Eddie Rickenbacker raced was a Firestone, manufactured by the Columbus Buggy Company in 1907.

IRISH BROADWAY

Irish immigrants in Columbus had formed an independent community centered near today's Arena District. They came to work on canals and later the railroads and settled in an area that came to be affectionately known as "Irish Broadway," a bustling area situated just south of Union Depot on Naghten Street, between St. Patrick Church on the east and the Irish hotels, saloons and shops along High Street on the west. By the 1900s however, second and third generation Irish-Americans had already "moved up" to other areas of the city and the area began its shift toward strictly commercial uses. During excavation for the Nationwide Arena in 1998, a trove of various artifacts from this period was found, including bottles, railroad tracks and telegraph lines.

Billy Naghten

Today known as Nationwide Boulevard, this thoroughfare was originally known as North Public Lane before being renamed Naghten Street in honor of William "Billy" Naghten, a notable, colorful figure of Irish heritage who served as president of Columbus City Council from 1863 until his death in 1870. Because there were no zoning codes, areas that were once primarily residential soon gave way to commercial and industrial concerns.

An Ohio Bicentennial Historical Marker was erected in McFerson Commons in 2002 to commemorate contributions of the Irish Community in the building of Columbus.

PA Egan Undertaking and Livery

Horse-drawn hearses were in common use when Patrick Egan opened his Undertaking and Livery business at 26 W. Naghten Street in 1859. Egan, who also served as Franklin County Coroner, was the founder of the Egan-Ryan funeral services company that is still in family hands today. Today the site is the grassy area at the northwest corner of North High Street and West Nationwide Boulevard, home to the Bicentennial Perennial Garden across from the Hyatt Regency Hotel.

St. Patrick Church

St. Patrick Church, a Roman Catholic place of worship, was home to the first English-speaking Catholic congregation in the city. Columbus' Irish Catholics had worshiped at the predominantly German-speaking Holy Cross Church on South Fifth Street prior to construction of St. Patrick, which was dedicated on September 25, 1853. A fire in 1935 nearly destroyed everything. However, the exterior brick walls survived and the church was reopened in 1936. It is located at 376 E. Naghten Street and is known for its two matching, low crenelated towers that flank the entrance.

Beals Job Wagon Line

Beals Job Wagon Line, another Irish-American owned business, occupied this building at 23 East Naghten Street, which today is the site of Sensenbrenner Park. The park, located at the southeast corner of North High Street and East Nationwide Boulevard, was dedicated in 1980 to M.E. "Jack" Sensenbrenner, who served as Mayor of Columbus from 1954 to 1959 and 1964 to 1971.

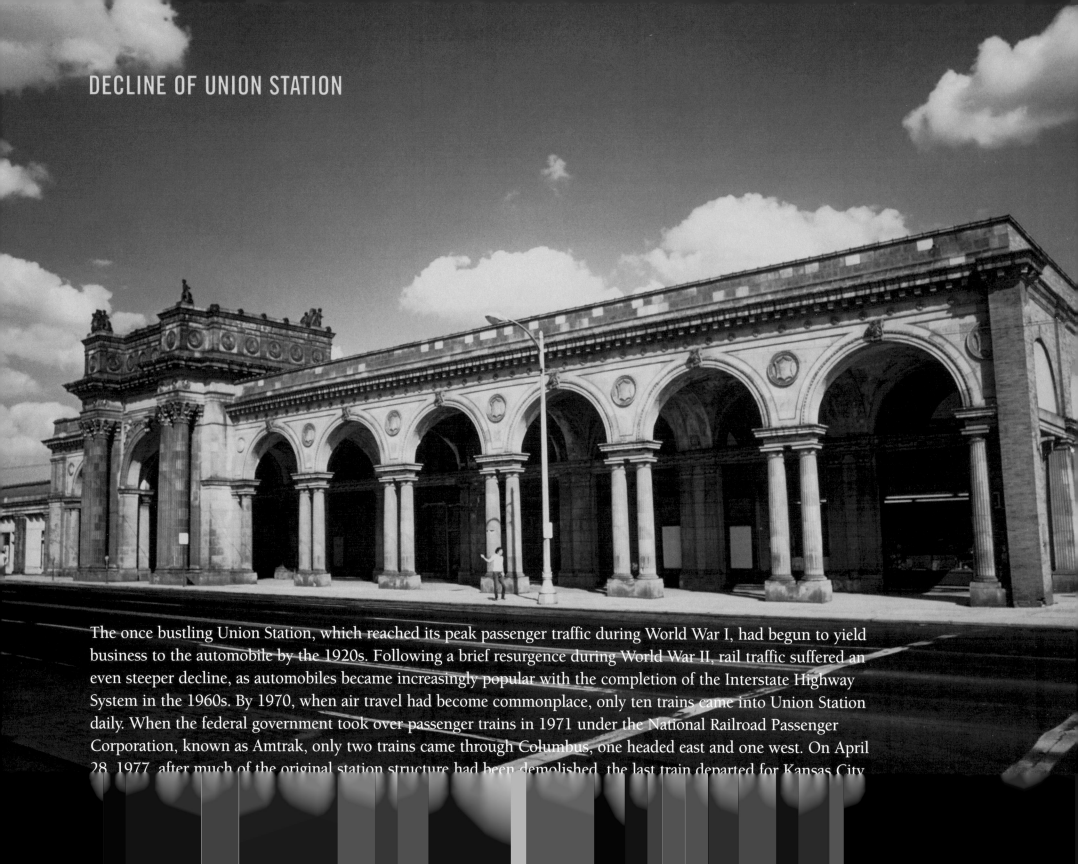

The once bustling Union Station, which reached its peak passenger traffic during World War I, had begun to yield business to the automobile by the 1920s. Following a brief resurgence during World War II, rail traffic suffered an even steeper decline, as automobiles became increasingly popular with the completion of the Interstate Highway System in the 1960s. By 1970, when air travel had become commonplace, only ten trains came into Union Station daily. When the federal government took over passenger trains in 1971 under the National Railroad Passenger Corporation, known as Amtrak, only two trains came through Columbus, one headed east and one west. On April 28, 1977, after much of the original station structure had been demolished, the last train departed for Kansas City.

Listed in the National Register of Historic Places, the Beaux-Arts Classicism-style Union Station Arcade, which once sat atop the High Street viaduct where the Hyatt Regency Hotel stands today, was derelict by the 1970s. A pedestrian traverses the Arcade sidewalk in front of boarded openings that were once entrances to shops.

The interior of Union Station — seen here at the track level just before it was closed — had beautifully arched corridors lined by paired Beaux-Arts pilasters and topped by a coffered ceiling. Each coffer was graced with a molded-plaster rosette, which added to the sense of warmth and character.

In the late 1970s, plans were underway for a new convention center near the historic Union Station. Initially, plans called for incorporating the arcade facade in the new facility. Without public discussion and for reasons still unexplained today however, demolition of the city-owned structure began after dark on Friday, October 22, 1976. The event is referred to by local preservationists as "the Friday Night massacre."

DESTRUCTION OF UNION STATION

Only the north pavilion arch of the once graceful Union Station Arcade remained standing amid the rubble. One Nationwide Plaza, built in 1976, can be seen behind and to the left of the arch.

Saving a Piece of History

Concerned citizens rallied to save one of Columbus' most recognizable landmarks. By obtaining a temporary injunction overnight, demolition was successfully halted, albeit temporarily. This construction worker is part of a crew that dismantled what was left of one of the arcade's two arches, until a new home could be found for it.

Arch Park

One of the two arches that were key features of the Union Station arcade is all that was spared from the wrecking ball. A group of preservation-minded citizens had painstakingly rebuilt the arch at its new home dubbed "Arch Park," which was dedicated in 1980. Located at Marconi Boulevard and Hickory Alley, several blocks from its original location on the east side of High Street, the arch remained here until it was moved to its present location in McFerson Commons. Today a parking garage stands on the arch's temporary home.

BECOMING A MODERN CITY

Construction of the Hyatt Regency continued a tradition of upscale lodging in the area. In earlier days, the Davidson, Deshler and Chittenden were known as downtown luxury hotels that served thousands visiting the capital city. Today, the Hyatt Regency is one of the state's largest hotels and features meeting space, restaurants and 631 guest rooms.

The Hyatt Regency Hotel, which stands on the site of Columbus' first train depot, was completed in 1979 as part of the Ohio Center, Columbus' first convention facility. Although the hotel was financed through private monies, the Battelle Memorial Foundation formed a quasi-public entity to provide $36.5 million to build the convention facility as a charitable project for public benefit. The Ohio Center, at 400 North High Street, was the forerunner of today's Greater Columbus Convention Center. Although only 85,000 square feet, the Ohio Center was hailed as a point of civic pride. However, it was quickly seen as too small to keep up with Columbus' booming growth. Originally, the Ohio Center was to have incorporated the beautiful Union Station Arcade into its design, as it was intended to be an important part of a new regional transportation terminal. Convention goers were to have accessed trains at track level, as well as light rail service and buses providing convenient transit to the airport.

Downtown's changing face is seen here in the late 1970s. This site at Nationwide Boulevard and High Street, once home to Union Station's warehouses and freight facilities, was temporarily occupied with parking lots before construction of the Ohio Center.

NATIONWIDE

At the same time planning was underway for the convention facility on the north side of Naghten Boulevard, Nationwide Mutual Insurance Company began planning a modern high-rise office tower and public plaza for the south side of the street. There was considerable discussion about moving the company's headquarters far north to Delaware County. However, Dean Jeffers, then general chairman, wanted Nationwide to remain downtown where it could serve as a strong, vibrant contributor to the growing Columbus community. Construction of both the Ohio Center and One Nationwide Plaza were important because the area, once a bustling warehouse and transportation hub, was blighted by widespread areas of industrial, commercial and residential deterioration and obsolescence which had begun in the 1950s.

Groundbreaking for One Nationwide Plaza took place on July 12, 1974 at the corner of High Street and Nationwide Boulevard. The 40-story, 1,328,000 square foot tower and related garages, walkways and green space was seen as a catalyst for the remarkable rebirth of the surrounding area, including the Short North, as art galleries, retail establishments and restaurants began to pepper the neighborhood. Nationwide employees first occupied the new building on December 6, 1976; the 18-story Two Nationwide Plaza was completed in 1981; and in 1988 Three Nationwide Plaza topped out at 27 stories.

The Ohio Farm Bureau Federation, a consumer group organized by Ohio farmers, started what would become Nationwide in 1925. After rapid growth and several office moves, the insurer settled in this downtown Columbus building, dedicated in 1951. After the company's move to One Nationwide Plaza, the old building became home to the Ohio Department of Health.

CONVENTION CENTER

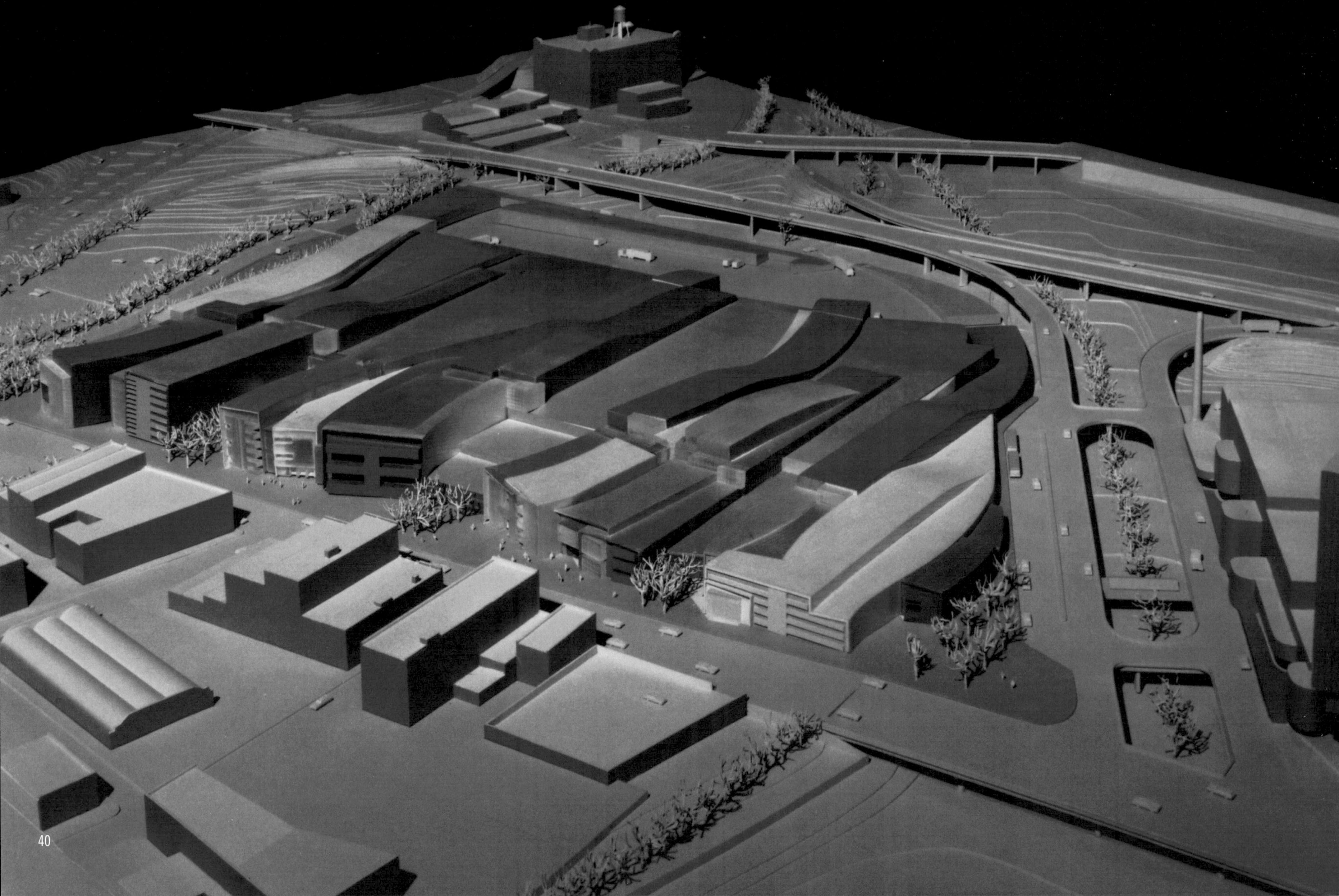

As convention industry in the capital city began to grow, it soon became obvious that the Ohio Center could no longer accommodate the burgeoning business. In 1993, the Greater Columbus Convention Center was built just north of, and connecting with, the Ohio Center. This unique, 600,000 square foot structure was designed by Peter Eisenman in his signature Deconstructivist style. His fragmented forms, oddly canted angles, colliding planes and variety of volumes characterize the $43 million center at 400 North High Street. The custom carpet of the interior, designed with a central axis that runs the length of the structure, is similarly broken up, creating vertigo for some visitors. A 1999 expansion brought the space to 1.7 million square feet.

A bird's-eye-view of the Greater Columbus Convention Center illustrates its resemblance to the train yard which once occupied the land near where it stands.

Peter Eisenman

Known as one of the foremost practitioners of Deconstructivist architecture in the United States, Peter Eisenman designed Columbus' Wexner Center for the Arts, as well as the Greater Columbus Convention Center. His prominence began as a member of the "New York Five," whose work was exhibited at the Museum of Modern Art in 1969. His unique style is often said to "liberate" architectural form, confounding user expectations through surprising, and often antagonistic space planning. In a similar vein, Eisenman's work alternately – or simultaneously – leaves visitors pleasantly surprised and profoundly confused.

The First Markets

In the pre-war days before the rise of suburbs and supermarkets, Columbus was home to four thriving public markets. Fishmongers, greengrocers, farmers and other merchants hawked their goods in open-air booths at the North, West, East and Central Markets. The original North End Market House, shown here in the 1920s, served the densely populated near-north neighborhoods from its location at 59 Spruce Street.

The Quonset Hut

In 1948, the original North End Market House burned to the ground. Shortly afterward, resilient North Market merchants pooled their resources and set up shop in this World War II surplus Quonset hut. The hut would be home to the merchants for nearly 50 years. During that period however, population centers and shopping habits changed, resulting in declining business, as the market became more novelty than necessity.

Today's North Market

The 1980s saw a national renewed interest in public markets, as well as revitalization of the Short North area and Greater Columbus Convention Center. In 1995, the North Market experienced a renaissance, this time in a turn-of-the-century warehouse. Today, the North Market is Columbus' only surviving public market, serving as a neighborhood anchor and featuring merchants ranging from modern gourmet grocers to traditional butchers, bakers and candle makers.

The first North Market opened in 1876 on land that had once been the city's North Graveyard. Located at what was once the northernmost border of Columbus, the graveyard closed in 1864. It took nearly a dozen years to clear the cemetery, as family members had their loved ones' remains relocated to the "country" in Greenlawn Cemetery and elsewhere. In 2001, construction workers installing a sewer line uncovered the remains of those who had been left behind. These were later reburied by the city at Greenlawn.

Battleship Building

An exterior of riveted steel is the distinguishing feature for the aptly named Battleship Building at 444 North Front Street. This photograph, taken from Park Street, shows the Battleship Building in an earlier incarnation as home to the Renard Linoleum & Rug Company. Listed on the National Register of Historic Places, it has been renovated and today provides hip urban condominium housing and office space adjacent to the North Market.

Greek Orthodox Cathedral

In 1910, thirty Columbus families of Greek heritage formed the Annunciation Greek Orthodox Cathedral. In March of 1922, they held their first service in this chapel, which today is part of the beautiful cathedral complex, completed in 1990.

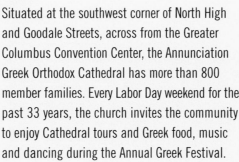

Goodale Park

The Lincoln Goodale monument was dedicated in 1888 in memory of Dr. Lincoln Goodale, who started one of the city's first private medical practices. He was also a dry goods merchant, a city councilman and city recorder. The land that is now Goodale Park, just north of Interstate 670, was donated by Dr. Goodale on November 11, 1851 and became the city's first recreation area. The land surrounding Goodale Park became a highly sought residential area. During the Civil War, Goodale Park was temporarily renamed Camp Jackson and served as a mobilization and training center.

Situated at the southwest corner of North High and Goodale Streets, across from the Greater Columbus Convention Center, the Annunciation Greek Orthodox Cathedral has more than 800 member families. Every Labor Day weekend for the past 33 years, the church invites the community to enjoy Cathedral tours and Greek food, music and dancing during the Annual Greek Festival.

1997 - THE PRESENT

DIAMOND IN THE ROUGH

For more than a decade after the Ohio Penitentiary officially closed its doors, the future of the 22-acre pen site and surrounding area looked bleak. The area seemed far removed from the city's core and detached from renewal efforts on downtown's northern edge.

With the exception of surface parking lots and a few isolated bars, this barren land sat vacant. And because many structures in the 150-year-old prison complex were crumbling, the area was dangerous as well. In 1994, a portion of the pen's outer wall fell, crushing two parked cars that fortunately were unoccupied. This calamity precipitated razing of the outer walls that year.

At the same time, it had become evident that the city needed an arena to capture the many concerts, ice shows and sporting events that were bypassing Columbus for other cities. But paying for an arena would prove difficult. Throughout the 1980s, several ballot initiatives to raise taxes to finance an arena complex were turned down by voters. Private developers felt that without a major tenant to occupy the space, an arena would be unprofitable. As one official said at the time, "Everyone wants an arena, but no one wants to pay for it."

A MAJOR LEAGUE CITY

In 1997, Franklin County voters were again presented with a tax package that would partially finance a sports complex on the long vacant pen site. The private sector was to finance the remainder of the cost.

However, the ballot initiative failed.

Within days, a determined Nationwide Insurance quickly assembled a plan to make a Columbus arena a reality. Nationwide announced plans to develop Nationwide Arena, a 20,000-seat venue at the corner of Nationwide Boulevard and Front Street. Nationwide Arena would be among the few privately-financed civic arenas in the nation.

Coinciding with the new arena would be a National Hockey League franchise to call it home. After 25 years of planning and dreaming, Columbus "joined the majors" when the NHL granted the city an expansion team license—one of only four awarded that year. NHL officials cited the city's youthful population, healthy economy and continued growth as factors in winning the expansion.

The Blue Jackets Are Born!

The Columbus Blue Jackets' name is a nod to Ohio soldiers who served in the Union Army during the Civil War. More Ohio men per capita fought on the Union side than any other state in the North.

The team's color combination – patriotic red, federal blue and lime green – is unique in the NHL. Blue is the predominate color in recognition of the corporate colors of the three companies instrumental in gaining Columbus a place in the NHL: Worthington Industries, Wolfe Enterprises and Nationwide Insurance.

The name was selected by the National Hockey League from among nearly 14,000 entries submitted during a "name the new team" contest sponsored by Wendy's. Seven individuals submitted the winning name. The team's first game was played against the Chicago Blackhawks in October, 2000.

More than 4,000 enthusiastic hockey fans rallied downtown to celebrate the news of Columbus' new ice hockey team.

"An insect with an attitude," is how the new National Hockey League expansion team's mascot was described when the team's name was introduced to the community in 1997. Dubbed "Stinger," the mascot is a feisty lime-green bug, wearing a blue Union Army jacket and cap and wielding a hockey stick. Stinger is said to embody the attitude of a city that is fast, aggressive, teamwork-oriented, industrious, hard-working and young – Columbus!

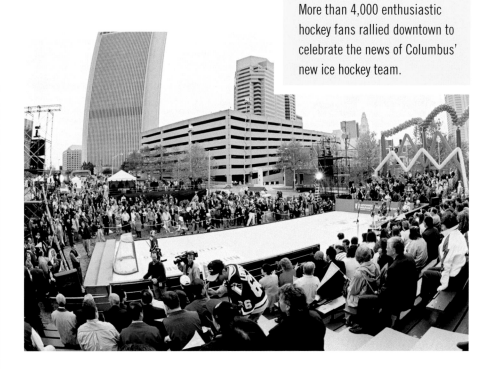

A NEW URBAN NEIGHBORHOOD

An initial tour of seven other cities' sports arenas was intended to distill for Columbus an amalgam of the best elements from each design. Instead, the survey made it clear that Ohio's capital city must be graced with something completely different, even unpredictable.

Rather than build an arena isolated from the city's surroundings, officials developed a holistic plan to transform the entire area into a lively neighborhood. The Arena District was born.

The objective was simple: create an extension of the city's urban fabric that fits with the surroundings. Encompassing the former penitentiary site and surrounding area, the Arena District would include 75 acres of offices, housing, restaurants and entertainment venues. The design of the area would seamlessly integrate new and old buildings with city streets, sidewalks and public gathering places.

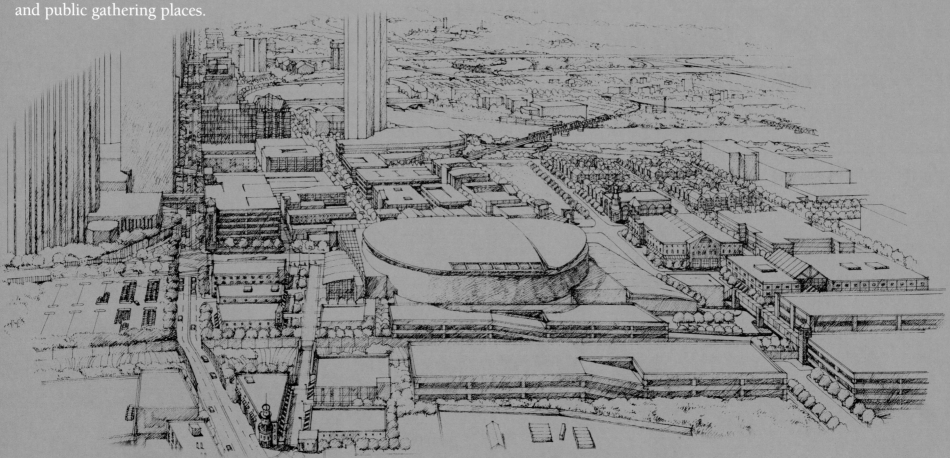

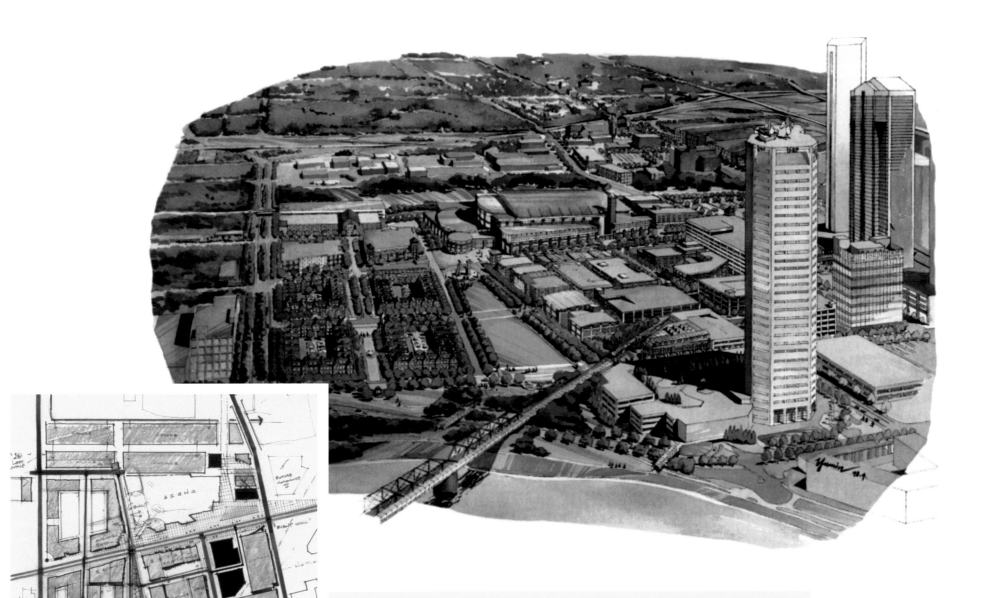

The Arena District's master plan is the guideline for the area's evolution. The Arena District of today has not diverged much from this initial sketch developed by planning firm MSI in 1997. Planners made intentional decisions to expand downtown by connecting the area to the High Street corridor on the east and the riverfront on the south.

BOLD VISIONS

Excitement and energy were as integral to the master plan as bricks and mortar. To envision how the Arena District would come to life, Nationwide called upon four local architectural firms, including Acock Associates, 360 Architecture (formerly Heinlein Schrock), David Benjamin Meleca Architecture and Jonathan Barnes Architecture and Design.

Taking cues from the best urban neighborhoods in the world, the architects dreamt of a place where people strolled brick sidewalks, dined alfresco under the stars and gathered for big special events.

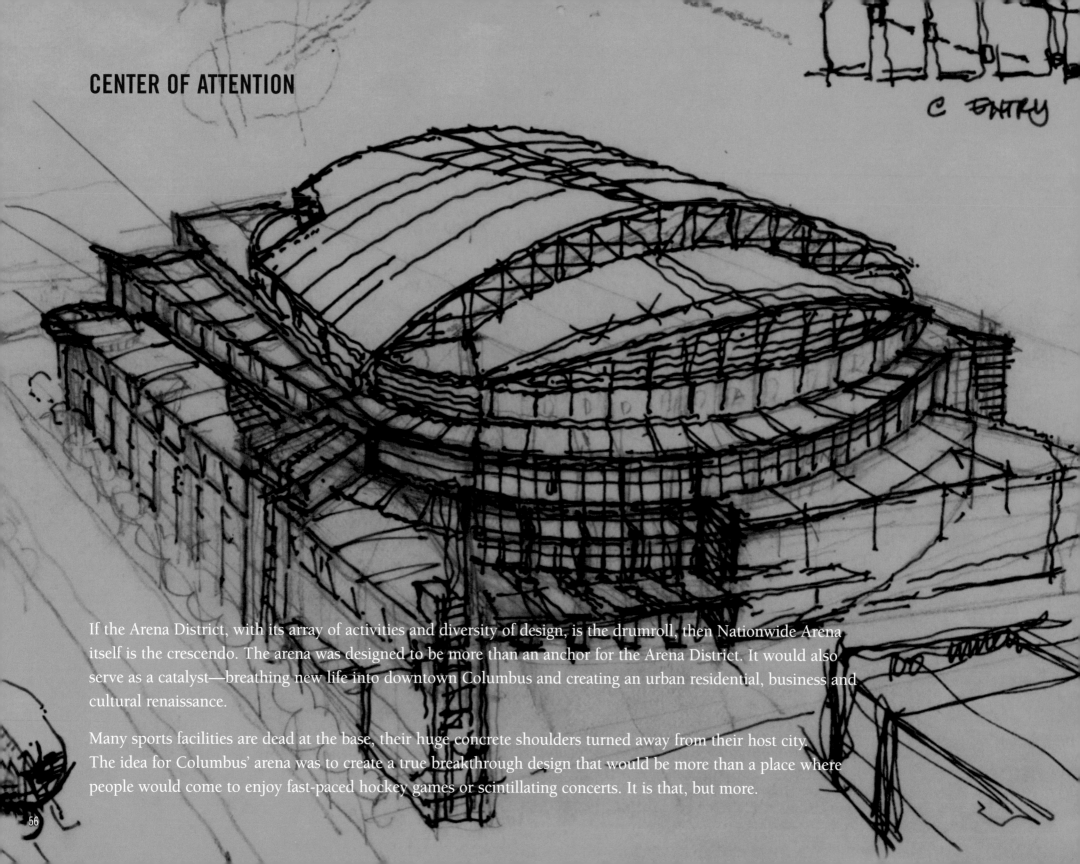

CENTER OF ATTENTION

If the Arena District, with its array of activities and diversity of design, is the drumroll, then Nationwide Arena itself is the crescendo. The arena was designed to be more than an anchor for the Arena District. It would also serve as a catalyst—breathing new life into downtown Columbus and creating an urban residential, business and cultural renaissance.

Many sports facilities are dead at the base, their huge concrete shoulders turned away from their host city. The idea for Columbus' arena was to create a true breakthrough design that would be more than a place where people would come to enjoy fast-paced hockey games or scintillating concerts. It is that, but more.

Nationwide Arena is not the behemoth usually expected in sports venues. Because the site slopes to the west, part of the interior is actually underground, creating a human-friendly scale and proportion that fits with the surrounding neighborhood of the Arena District.

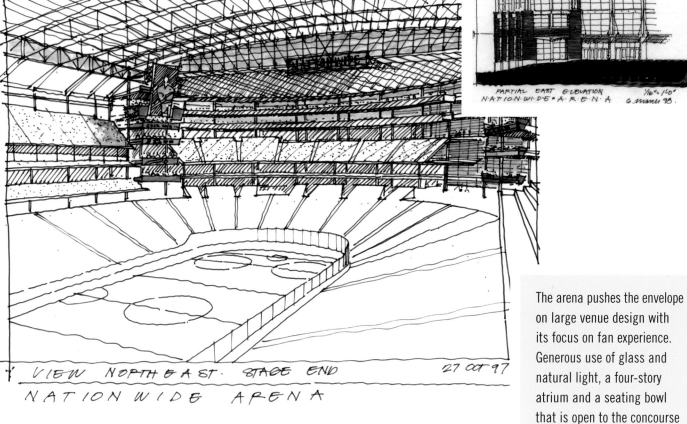

PARTIAL EAST ELEVATION   1/16" = 1'-0"
N·A·T·I·O·N·WI·DE·A·R·E·N·A   6 MARCH 98.

VIEW NORTHEAST. STAGE END   27 OCT 97
N A T I O N W I D E   A R E N A

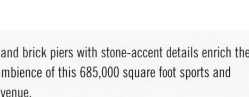

The arena pushes the envelope on large venue design with its focus on fan experience. Generous use of glass and natural light, a four-story atrium and a seating bowl that is open to the concourse connect fans to the action the minute they enter the building.

Terrazzo floors and brick piers with stone-accent details enrich the extraordinary ambience of this 685,000 square foot sports and entertainment venue.

PREMIER ENTERTAINMENT, INSIDE AND OUT

The Arena District is about more than just Nationwide Arena itself. It's about the synergy of urban living, downtown working and city nightlife coming together to create unique connections that soothe, inspire and electrify the senses – often all at the same time.

Constructed after the Arena's opening, the Arena Grand Theatre and Lifestyle Communities Pavilion diversify the Arena District's entertainment offerings and contribute to around-the-clock activity.

Arena Grand Theatre

The early twentieth-century movie palaces that once graced downtown influenced the design of the Arena Grand Theatre, Columbus' first urban theatre built since 1928. Dramatic staircases and balcony seating are combined with modern luxuries such as a club lounge, premium leather chairs and a small screening room. These details and the area's dense infrastructure led architects to create a unique vertical theatre with auditoriums on three levels. Clean, understated design intentionally allows the movie to be the star of the show.

PEN-WEST PAVILION 10·18·00

Lifestyle Communities Pavilion

Formerly known as PromoWest Pavilion, Lifestyle Communities Pavilion brings live music to the Arena District throughout the year. The first indoor/outdoor music venue in the nation features a unique reversible stage design. During summer months, music fans fill a bowl-shaped lawn and enjoy the city skyline as a backdrop. But as the temperature drops or when weather turns for the worse, the stage is reversed and musicians perform in an intimate 2,200 seat venue.

The Arena District was designed to bring pedestrian activity back to Columbus' urban core.

Before the development of the Arena District, a walk from the Scioto River through downtown into the Short North was hardly inviting. Parking lots, dark warehouses and remains of the Ohio Penitentiary littered the landscape.

Today, that same path is now a civilized stroll where patrons discover tightly-knit infrastructure, street-level architectural detail and wandering walkways.

The spine of the Arena District is Nationwide Boulevard. Wide brick sidewalks, punctuated by inviting green spaces and hospitable storefronts create a comfortable buffer between walkers and the smooth flow of street traffic.

ADTV — Arena District Television — along with rotating billboards, kiosks and other graphic elements create movement and life that energizes, engages and stimulates district visitors.

Fanciful and fierce, the Columbus Blue Jackets' mascot, Stinger, takes the form of a stone gargoyle to stand guard over the Arena Crossing walkway. The whimsical touch was a surprise addition to the 401 N. Front Street building by Acock Associates.

Turn-of-the-century brick pavers that once made the foundation of Naghten, Maple and West streets now add detail, texture and a bit of history to the Arena District. Most of the bricks were originally manufactured and shipped from Ohio's Hocking Valley —then the region's brick and clay capital. Some still remain branded by then-prominent brick manufacturers, including Nelson-ville Brick of Nelsonville, Ohio.

After construction of Nationwide Arena, the bricks were cleaned and moved by hand into this alley, known as Arena Crossing.

TIMELESS DESIGN

Will the people like it? It may be simple, but that was the question that guided building design in the Arena District.

Too often, architects stress form over function in creating obscure buildings that may win design awards, but lose the popular vote. Here, architects deliberately applied familiar materials such as brick and glass in timeless designs that create warm, contemporary spaces.

And by drawing on the creativity of more than one architect, a diversity of design is woven into the urban fabric.

Details such as granite curbs and brick streets not only add street-level beauty. Their high quality ensures the Arena District is a neighborhood that will stand the test of time.

Steel beams and rivets are a reminder of the turn-of-the-century warehouses and factories that once occupied the area.

Both contemporary and clean, glass offers natural light and transparency. Office workers, hockey fans and restaurant patrons alike are invited to take in the beauty of their surroundings, both inside and out.

Rich red brick dominates the Arena District. The material is not only warm and historic, but creates a feeling of strength and permanence.

PAST MEETS PRESENT

During construction of Nationwide Arena, care was taken to preserve historic structures that were feet from the new building. The effect is a determined cohesiveness, as architectural design of the new nods to the industrial heritage of the past. Nineteenth-century brick warehouses – richly detailed – are complemented by new structures that echo, but don't copy, the traditional architecture.

Ohio Moline Plow

Once home to Ohio's largest distributor of farm equipment, the Ohio Moline Plow building is one of the few remaining examples of wholesaling and warehousing architecture in Columbus. Built in 1913 and renovated in 1998, the building was adapted to fit the needs of modern office and restaurant space without making significant structural changes. The interior features a loft-like atmosphere with 12-foot high ceilings and large barbell-shaped columns throughout. The structure was added to the National Register of Historic Places in 1998.

Acock Associates

This former 1923 warehouse, now known as the Acock building, was renovated in 1987 by Acock Associates, the architectural firm it now houses. Located at 383 N. Front Street, the building now features 30,000 square feet of office space. Loading docks on the east side of the building were renovated to become ground-level door-ways and exterior brick walls were replaced with floor-to-ceiling arched windows.

New life flourishes, supported by remnants of the past. Heavy iron cell doors, discarded from the Ohio Penitentiary, become trellises for flowering pyracantha and ivy outside of the Ohio Moline Plow building.

Limestone from the Ohio Penitentiary has been recycled in select structures throughout the Arena District. These pieces of the past can be found in exterior walls at the Arena Grand Theatre and Burnham Square caretaker's house as well as in retaining walls along North Bank Park walking paths.

UNION STATION ARCH

Quite possibly the most concrete representation of past mingling with present is the historic Union Station Arch. Once a part of the landmark beaux-arts arcade at Columbus' Union Station, the arch has taken on new life as the centerpiece of McFerson Commons. The arch is not only an icon of the Arena District, but has become a landmark for the City of Columbus and its people.

This historically significant piece of Columbus' heritage was not easy to move. Because it had been disassembled stone by stone when it was rescued from the wrecking ball in 1976, the then new mortar with which it had been reassembled was still strong. The soft, terra-cotta enhanced arch would have to be moved in one piece.

Over a period of several days in March 1999, the arch was slowly and meticulously moved from its temporary home at Front and Hickory Streets to the apex of McFerson Commons.

The 660-ton arch was lifted and moved by the same company that moved the Cape Hatteras Lighthouse. As the arch was rolled — inch by inch — over the railroad tracks and down the slight incline of Nationwide Boulevard, its excruciatingly slow, yet regal, progress to its new foundation was barely perceptible. Columbusites who wanted to see history in the making flocked to observe its measured advance.

Today, the arch designed by famous architect Daniel Burnham is an icon of enduring grace, style and strength. A broad granite stripe, set into the plaza in front of the arch, indicates the distance this architectural heirloom once sat from the curb at its original location on High Street.

GREEN SPACES AND GATHERING PLACES

In the Arena District, ample green space and public gathering areas offer a soft balance to buildings and architectural hardscapes. They are a magnet for human activity, providing a collective sense of place to congregate, relax or rejuvenate.

North Bank Park

The Scioto River is the main attraction of North Bank Park, dedicated in 2005. Pedestrians are drawn from the Arena District, across Spring and Long streets via a wide, low, and welcoming gateway that leads to a beautiful glass and brick pavilion, fountain and plaza overlooking the Columbus city skyline, and just steps away from the replica Santa Maria. A paved bike and walking path transects the park, allowing visitors to follow the river from Worthington on the north to Whittier Peninsula on the south.

McFerson Commons

As the master plan was being developed, McFerson Commons was the key element that would link the bustle and activity of the Arena District to the riverfront. The park was also a catalyst for continued riverfront development, including North Bank Park. Today, the three-acre mallway provides a cooling respite and serves as a common "backyard playground" for the urban neighborhood.

Battelle Plaza

Originally called Celebration Square, Battelle Plaza is the vibrant heart of the Arena District. Located at the corner of Front Street and Nationwide Boulevard, it is also a welcome gateway to Nationwide Arena's main entrance, flooding with hockey and concert fans on event nights. The plaza itself plays host to several major events throughout the year, including concerts and charity walks and runs.

A PLACE TO CALL HOME

The Arena District is a neighborhood for people to work, play and live.

Even the earliest stages of the district's master plan included a residential component. While office workers come and go on the nine-to-five, apartment and condominium dwellers bring around-the-clock vitality to an area.

With the city's best sports, cultural and entertainment destinations literally steps away, residents here enjoy an urban lifestyle unlike anything else in the region.

Burnham Square Condominiums

Named for famed architect and urban planner Daniel Burnham, Burnham Square condominiums provide the first owner-occupied residential opportunity in the Arena District. Residents are treated to soaring city views and generous terrace and patio space. Nestled between the two-building development is an intimate courtyard called Burnham Square, featuring "the caretakers house," a service building constructed of limestone salvaged from the Ohio Penitentiary.

Arena Crossing Apartments

An old bridge that originally served a southern Ohio county road received a new life as a pedestrian walkway adjacent to the Arena Crossing Apartments. After being refurbished, the Arena Crossing bridge now provides a convenient link between the Arena District and the North Market area.

LIFE OF THE COMMUNITY

Just as this area was teeming with life and activity in the 1850s, today the Arena District is a gathering place for successive generations to live, work and play.

Columbus Blue Jackets

The exhilaration of 20,000 screaming hockey fans is reason enough to enjoy what the Arena District has to offer.

Red, White & Boom!

Crowds filling McFerson Commons catch a prime spot to watch Red, White and Boom!, Columbus' annual Independence Day fireworks celebration.

Columbus Marathon

Each autumn, runners from across the nation compete in the annual Columbus Marathon, a 26-mile race that ends in the Arena District.

Rockin' Eve

Each year, thousands of people ring in the New Year at the Arena District's Rockin' Eve celebration in Battelle Plaza.

PUBLICATION TEAM

Managing Editor: Michelle Chippas, Nationwide Realty Investors

Editor and Project Manager: Nathan Kraft, Nationwide Realty Investors

Publication Design: Scott Adams Design Associates

Copywriting: Jaron Terry, APR, Jaron Terry Communications

Research: Ed Lentz, Pastfinders

ACKNOWLEDGEMENTS

The production of this book would not have been possible without the tremendous help from the following individuals and organizations.

Scott Ralston, 360 Architecture

Brad Schrock, 360 Architecture

George Acock, Acock Associates Architecture

Chicago Historical Society

Jim Hunter and Linda Deitch, Columbus Dispatch

Marc Conte, Columbus Downtown Development Resource Center

Biography, History and Travel staff, The Columbus Metropolitan Library

George Arnold, H.R. Gray

William Habig, Mid Ohio Regional Planning Commission

Keith Myers, MSI

John Petrushka, MSI

Tom Griffin, Kim Rottmayer, Laura Sauer and Michelle Smith, Nationwide Corporate Photography team

Ohio Historical Society

Bob Loversidge, Jr., Schooley Caldwell Associates

PHOTO CREDITS

p. 8/9 Lithograph, Columbus in 1854, Columbus Metropolitan Library

p. 10 Ohio Penitentiary, Columbus Metropolitan Library

p. 11 Ohio Penitentiary (upper left), Columbus Metropolitan Library

p. 11 Ohio Penitentiary (lower right), Ohio Historical Society

p. 12 Ohio Penitentiary 1968 Riots, Columbus Dispatch Archives

p. 13 1930 Easter Monday Fire aftermath, Columbus Dispatch archives

p. 13 Death Chamber, Columbus Metropolitan Library

p. 14 Bankers' Row, Columbus Metropolitan Library

p. 14 Sam Sheppard, Columbus Dispatch archives

p. 15 John Hunt Morgan Cell, Columbus Dispatch archives

p. 15 O. Henry, Columbus Dispatch archives

p. 16 Ohio Penitentiary in 1977, Columbus Dispatch archives

p. 17 Ohio Penitentiary (prisoners leaving), Columbus Dispatch archives

p. 17 Ohio Penitentiary (lowering of flag), Columbus Dispatch archives

p. 17 Ohio Penitentiary (prisoners in file formation), Columbus Dispatch archives

p. 18 First union depot, Columbus Metropolitan Library

p. 19 Second union depot, Columbus Metropolitan Library

p. 20/21 Union Station, Columbus Dispatch archives

p. 22 Commuters in front of Union Station, Columbus Metropolitan Library, courtesy of Laura Mueller Kuhnert

p. 22 Daniel Burnham, Chicago Historical Society

p. 23 Davidson Hotel, Columbus Metropolitan Library

p. 23 North High Street looking north from viaduct, Columbus Metropolitan Library

p. 23 North High Street looking south from viaduct, Columbus Metropolitan Library

p. 24 Soldiers returning from Spanish American War, Columbus Dispatch Archives

p. 24 Woodrow Wilson at Union Station, Columbus Metropolitan Library

p. 25 Shriner's Parade, Columbus Metropolitan Library

p. 25 Lincoln's Casket, Columbus Metropolitan Library

p. 26 Warehouses around Union Station, Columbus Metropolitan Library

p. 26 55 E. Nationwide Blvd. (before and after photos), Columbus Metropolitan Library

p. 27 Former A&P Building, Robert Mullenix / Dunwanderin' Productions

p. 27 Dean & Barry Paint Co., Miriam Yenkin / Marconi Square

p. 28 Columbus Buggy Co., Columbus Metropolitan Library

p. 29 Iron Buggy Co., Columbus Metropolitan Library

p. 29 Combination Phaeton, Columbus Metropolitan Library

p. 29 Eddie Rickenbacker, Columbus Metropolitan Library

p. 30 B & O Freight Station, Columbus Metropolitan Library

p. 30 Irish Broadway historical marker, Matthew Roharik / Roharik Photographic

p. 31 PA Egan Undertaking and Livery, Columbus Metropolitan Library

p. 31 St. Patrick Church, Nationwide Corporate Photography

p. 31 Beals Job Wagon Line, Nationwide Corporate Photography

p. 32 Decline of Union Station, Nationwide Corporate Photography

p. 33 Union Station decaying interior (top images), Columbus Dispatch archives

p. 33 Union Station interior (lower image), Columbus Metropolitan Library

p. 34 Union Station arch, Columbus Dispatch archives

p. 35 Crane at arch, Columbus Dispatch archives

p. 35 Arch Park, Columbus Dispatch archives

p. 36 Hyatt Regency rendering, Columbus Chamber of Commerce

p. 37 Ohio Center, entrance sign and aerial photo, Columbus Dispatch archives

p. 37 North High Street and Nationwide Boulevard intersection, Nationwide Corporate Photography

p. 38 Nationwide Plaza I, Nationwide Corporate Photography

p. 39 Nationwide development (all images), Nationwide Corporate Photography

p. 40 Convention Center model, Columbus Dispatch archives

p. 41 Peter Eisenman, Columbus Dispatch archives

p. 41 Convention Center aerial, Columbus Dispatch archives

p. 42 First North Market, Columbus Dispatch archives

p. 43 Quonset Hut, Columbus Dispatch archives

p. 43 People shopping at market, Columbus Dispatch archives

p. 43 Today's North Market (before), Columbus Dispatch archives

p. 43 Today's North Market (after), Matthew Roharik / Roharik Photographic

p. 44 Battleship Building, Columbus Dispatch archives

p. 45 Greek Orthodox Cathedral (top image), Scott Adams

p. 45 Greek Orthodox Cathedral (lower image), Nationwide Corporate Photography

p. 45 Lincoln Goodale Monument, Scott Adams

p. 48/49 Arena District in 1997, Nationwide Corporate Photography

p. 50 Blue Jackets, Nationwide Corporate Photography

p. 51 Officials at Nationwide Arena announcement, Nationwide Corporate Photography

p. 51 Stinger, Columbus Blue Jackets

p. 51 Hockey Rally, Nationwide Corporate Photography

p. 52 Master plan, MSI Design

p. 53 Master plan watercolor, MSI Design

p. 53 Master plan, MSI Design

p. 54 Arena District conceptual rendering, Acock and Associates

p. 55 Arena District conceptual rendering (top), Meleca Architecture

p. 55 Arena District conceptual rendering (lower left), Acock and Associates

p. 55 Arena District conceptual rendering (lower right), Meleca Architecture

p. 56 Nationwide Arena sketch, 360 Architecture

p. 57 Nationwide Arena (all images), 360 Architecture

p. 58 Arena Grand Theatre sketch, 360 Architecture

p. 59 Arena Grand Theatre interior rendering, 360 Architecture

p. 59 Arena Grand Theatre photo, Nationwide Corporate Photography

p. 59 Lifestyle Communities Pavilion rendering, 360 Architecture

p. 59 Lifestyle Communities Pavilion photo, Nationwide Corporate Photography

p. 60 Arena Crossing walkway rendering, 360 Architecture

p. 60 Arena Crossing walkway photo, Matthew Roharik / Roharik Photographic

p. 61 Nationwide Arena and Nationwide Boulevard, Matthew Roharik / Roharik Photographic

p. 61 Stinger gargoyle, Nationwide Corporate Photography

p. 61 Battelle Plaza and ADTV, Nationwide Corporate Photography

p. 61 Cobblestone and exterior of Moline Plow building, Matthew Roharik / Roharik Photographic

p. 62 Nationwide Arena, Matthew Roharik / Roharik Photographic

p. 63 all images, Nationwide Corporate Photography

p. 64 Moline Plow building, Matthew Roharik / Roharik Photographic

p. 65 Moline Plow rendering, NBBJ Architecture

p. 65 Trellises, Robert Mullenix / Dunwanderin' Productions

p. 65 North Bank Park, Scott Adams

p. 65 383 N. Front Street, Matthew Roharik / Roharik Photographic

p. 66 Union Station Arch, Nationwide Corporate Photography

p. 67 Union Station Arch progressive photography, Nationwide Corporate Photography

p. 68 Kickball on McFerson Commons, Nationwide Corporate Photography

p. 69 McFerson Commons rendering, MSI Design

p. 69 McFerson Commons photo, Matthew Roharik / Roharik Photographic

p. 69 Battelle Plaza, Nationwide Corporate Photography

p. 69 North Bank Park, Nationwide Corporate Photography

p. 70 Arena Crossing Apartments rendering, 360 Architecture

p. 71 Burnham Square Condominiums caretakers' house, Matthew Roharik, Roharik Photographic

p. 71 Burnham Square Condominiums exterior, Matthew Roharik / Roharik Photographic

p. 71 Arena Crossing Apartments, Nationwide Corporate Photography

p. 71 Burnham Square Condominiums rendering, 360 Architecture

p. 72 Arena Grand Theatre exterior, Nationwide Corporate Photography

p. 73 Columbus Blue Jackets, Nationwide Corporate Photography

p. 73 Red, White and Boom!, Nationwide Corporate Photography

p. 73 Columbus Marathon, Nationwide Corporate Photography

p. 73 Arena District New Year's Rockin' Eve, Glen Pritchard

p. 74 Union Station Arch during Red, White & Boom!, Nationwide Corporate Photography

p. 78 Ohio State Penitentiary, 1952 Aerial, Columbus Dispatch archives

p. 79 Arena District, 2005 Aerial, Fly By Shootings

1952

BELMONT CASKETS
LEAD COATED STEEL

2005